Until You Say I Do

Jay and Diane Strack

A TRUE LOVE WAITS
RESOURCE

LifeWay Press
Nashville, Tennessee

✚

© Copyright 1997 • LifeWay Press
All rights reserved

Reprinted 1998

Item 5201-44

ISBN 0-7673-3181-8

Dewey Decimal Classification: 306.81
Subject Heading: Marriage

This book is the text for course GC-0211 in the subject area
Home/Family in the Christian Growth Study Plan.
Unless otherwise indicated, biblical quotations are from The Holy Bible,
New International Version, copyright © 1973, 1978, 1984 by
International Bible Society. Used by permission.

Verses marked KJV are taken from the *King James Version* of the Bible.
Verses marked TLB are taken from *The Living Bible.* Copyright © Tyndale
House Publishers, Wheaton, Illinois, 1971. Used by permission.

Verses marked NASB are from the *New American Standard Bible.* Copyright
© The Lockman Foundation, 1960, 1962, 1963, 1968, 1971, 1972,
1973, 1975, 1977. Used by permission.

Printed in the United States of America

LifeWay Press
Nashville, Tennessee

Youth Section
Discipleship and Family Division
LifeWay Christian Resources of the Southern Baptist Convention
127 Ninth Avenue, North, Nashville, TN 37234-0152

Contents

The Writers

Jay and Diane Strack have been married for 25 years and have two daughters. They both are committed to communicating the truth of God's Word to students. Jay is the founder of Jay Strack Evangelistic Association and is a nationally known communicator and author. For 20 years he has worked with students - face to face, on their own turf. He has led over 7,500 college, middle and high school assemblies. He is in touch with students and is the host of *N'-2-Livin'*, a weekly national radio program. He is an author and editor of the *Transformer Student Bible* and *The True Love Waits Bible*.

Introduction

The very title of this book, *Until You Say I Do*, implies thinking in the future tense. In other words, your dating life as a teen is moving toward an ultimate goal of marriage and family. Whom do you want to be when you get there? What type of person will you present to your future spouse? What will you pass on to your children? Right now, you are setting the stage for marriage, family, and your future.

The sessions of this book present scenarios you are probably familiar with either firsthand or as an observer of peers. The bottom line—life is the result of choices and the consequences or blessings that follow. This is particularly true in the area of dating and relationships in the teen years. Each chapter narrates a true story* and scriptural advice for that situation.

Session one reminds us to "Think in the Future Tense." Session two investigates "Firting with Temptation" and the power available to change your "want to's." The third session deals with the question "How Far Is Too Far?" Session four, "Is Sex Wrong If You're Really in Love?" offers food for thought and a serious look at marriage and beyond. In the last session, "Sex: Isn't Everybody Doing It?" you'll read the testimonies of other youth who have faced sexual temptation and come through strong. It can be done!

This book will not answer every question about your sexuality and your dating life, but it will provide you with principles and truth that you can apply in your everyday situations. These principles and truths only work when you are courageous enough to put them into practice.

Anytime you see this symbol 🏃 you will know that it is time for you to stop and react and write down some of your own thoughts. Be honest in your responses. It will cause you to look at your life in a positive way and **ENCOURAGE YOU TO LIVE FOR CHRIST**.

This is a book for you to enjoy. It is not designed for you to rush through, feel guilty for any areas you come up short in, and then run on to the next study. It is a book to help you to commit your life to obedience to Christ. If you fall short in any area of obedience, confess it to Christ, repent of your sin, and claim His promise of forgiveness *(I John 1:9)*

*Although these accounts are based on true stories, the names in Sessions One through Four have been changed to protect the innocent and the guilty.

SESSION ONE:

Think In the Future Tense

A famous artist once said, "I paint life the way I want it to be and the majority of the time it turns out that way." Wouldn't you like to be able to paint a portrait of your future? To know exactly what will happen and when? Well, it's not as far out as it seems. For most students, the "future" seems light years away, something that can always be corrected later. In reality, the future is happening right now, each day, as you go. Every decision you make brings about another choice for tomorrow. You are writing your future now.

 It's time to BEGIN TODAY by thinking about TOMORROW'S END RESULT.

God's wisdom is ready to steer your course into the future.

Answer HONESTLY these four GREAT QUESTIONS, and you'll find THE ANSWERS TO LIFE'S DECISIONS.

1. What rule book will be the authority for my life? Place a check beside it. *(Your rule book should be based on the absolute truth. Following it will allow you to always make the right choices for your life.)*

☐ Rule book of the opinion of the crowd.

☐ Rule book of the actions and suggestions of my friends.

☐ Rule book of the influence of my parents' beliefs.

☐ Rule book of the Holy Bible.

Now circle the rule book that you have been following. Are there differences in the consequences of following the rule book you checked and the rule book you circled? List the possible differences.

2. What will I do with my life? *(These are the goals you set for yourself in the area of career and serving God.)*

3. How much and what type of education or training do I need to accomplish my goals? *(What you do now will be a bridge to the next step.)*

4. Who will I spend my life with? *(Maybe you haven't met this person yet. What qualities are you looking for in your future mate? Check the ones that apply and add others if you want.)*

☐ **Honesty**   ☐ **Fun**

☐ **Nice-looking**   ☐ **Bathes often**

☐ **Has lots of money**

☐ **A growing Christian**   ☐ **Loyalty**

☐ **Responsible** ☐ **Hard working**

☐ **Other** _____

As a Christian you already know this, but as a reminder:

 ALL of YOU belongs to Jesus.

YOUR SOUL—*In him we have redemption through his blood, the forgiveness of sins, in accordance with the riches of God's grace (Eph. 1:7).*

No, that's not the kind of soul that we are talking about here. This would be a sole. We are talking about your being that lives forever. Your soul!

YOUR BODY—*Do you not know that your body is a temple of the Holy Spirit, who is in you, whom you have received from God? You are not your own; you were bought at a price. Therefore honor God with your body (1 Cor. 6:19,20).*

Yes, the one you are thinking that it is. All of you that is physical.

YOUR WILL—*It is God's will that you should be sanctified: that you should avoid sexual immorality (1 Thess. 4:3).*

This *will* is the part of you that helps you determine how you live. It is the core of your decision maker.

John and Heidi

John pledged to remain pure at a True Love Waits rally and was known at school for his commitment to Christ. By the time he reached the eleventh grade, the guys were teasing him about being a virgin, and John started to have second thoughts. He went to a few parties after the football games, hoping it would help him fit in better at school and to be more accepted by his classmates. Gradually, John started making wrong choices by putting himself and his immediate desires first. He lost his commitment to Christ bit-by-bit. He stopped thinking so much about his future, his college plans, and the immediate and future consequences of poor choices. John was more interested in his newfound popularity. Having girls chase him was exciting and flattering.

Describe a time you tried to "fit in" a group by doing something that you were not comfortable with, and then you gradually began to feel more comfortable in the group.

John accepted a date with Heidi whose reputation for sleeping around was pretty well known. He thought it would be fun to experiment with things he'd read in teen magazines and seen in movies. In the theater of his mind, John anticipated a long make-out session, but told himself it would never go farther. Heidi had other ideas and accepted a dare from some of the football players to "see if she could bring John down."

She brought along some beer and, a few drinks later, convinced John to go to his house while no one was home. John agreed as the fantasies played in his mind, still intending to just "fool around." The alcohol won out. John was unprepared for what happened next. His parents returned unexpectedly and walked in as John and Heidi were having sex. John was embarrassed and humiliated.

Of course, the next day at school the news was out (headlines say, **JOHN SLEEPS WITH HEIDI**) and John's reputation as a Christian was destroyed. What he imagined would make him popular, instead caused him to be the laughing stock of the school. His parents felt they could no longer trust him and were deeply hurt.

&

And above all else, a subsequent trip to the doctor confirmed John's fear— Heidi had passed on genital herpes which could never be fully cured.

DATING—Does it have to be that difficult? Not really. Use the WHO, WHY, WHERE, WHAT and WILL test to keep your social life out of storms & into smooth sailing.

Here we go. Using John and Heidi's story as a guide, answer the following questions.

WHO is this person? Do I know his or her beliefs about moral purity? Are we moving toward the same goals in life?

In John's case, the answer was a definite **NO!** Remember, just because someone asks you out doesn't mean you have to go. Be secure enough in yourself to hang out in groups or with same-sex friends at events.

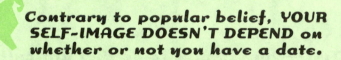

Contrary to popular belief, YOUR SELF-IMAGE DOESN'T DEPEND on whether or not you have a date.

WHY am I interested in dating him or her? Did the relationship begin as a friendship or a physical attraction?

Heidi was definitely a physical attraction, and a dangerous one at that. Never be flattered that someone is willing to use your body, or theirs for that matter. Dating should be fun, and viewed as preparation for marriage. In short, **DON'T DATE ANYONE YOU WOULDN'T MARRY.** This one rule can save you tons of heartache. Begin with friendship and trust God for the rest.

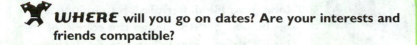 **WHERE** will you go on dates? Are your interests and friends compatible?

Over and over again, I hear stories of students who gave in to temptation because they were simply in the wrong place and surrounded by the wrong people. When you're at a party where other couples are making out, where drugs or alcohol are being used, you throw temptation at yourself—you become your own worst enemy.

The Bible tells us to *flee from sexual immorality (1 Cor. 6:18)*. Run as far away as you can, as fast as you can—keep your distance from anyone or any activity that could cause you to weaken your decision to remain sexually pure and compromise your commitment to Christ.

WHAT can I expect as a result of this relationship? How will I be challenged and changed by this person's influence on me?

John gave Heidi permission to influence his beliefs, and to change the course of his life's direction. When you do decide to date someone, *ask a lot of questions* first. Find out where he or she is headed in life and prayerfully decide if you should be under that influence.

WILL this choice honor my parents and God? Will it strengthen my goals and motivate me to stay on track?

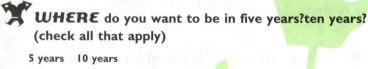

John's goals had one-by-one gone by the wayside. He forgot the **END** and began living for **TODAY**. Don't rush it.

You must remind yourself that God has the PERFECT PLAN.

Take the long look at life.

WHERE do you want to be in five years? ten years? (check all that apply)

5 years	10 years	
☐	☐	out of high school
☐	☐	involved in college/trade school
☐	☐	in prison
☐	☐	performing on Broadway
☐	☐	right where **God** wants me to be
☐	☐	in politics
☐	☐	in a foreign country as a missionary
☐	☐	other _____

These are not all the choices we could consider, but one thing we must consider now is that each choice we make today effects our tomorrow.

A TURNING POINT is when a significant change takes place in our lives. Turning points can have immediate or long-term time frames.

The significant change may not seem significant at the time. Your choice may be to take a first drink of alcohol, making it easier to take the second drink of alcohol the next time you are tempted, or your choice may be to say no to premarital sex, making it easier to say no the second time you are tempted.

People in the Bible also had turning points. These turning points, affected their futures—some immediately, some in the future. In some cases they may have realized the effect it could have on their future or in other cases, they gave no thought of the consequences of their choice and didn't think about the future.

For instance, take a look at this familiar story in *2 Samuel 11*.
DAVID was so consumed by lust for Bathsheba, that he committed adultery with her, *(thinking he could get away with it)* got her pregnant *(now they have another problem)*, and then devised a scheme to have her husband, Uriah killed in battle. After Bathsheba's time of mourning, David took her to be his wife. The child conceived out of marriage died and they later had more children who caused them some serious family problems. After David's confession of his sin, God forgave him, but he and Bathsheba suffered the consequences of their sin for life. What you do today, will effect your tomorrow. Just ask David. *(Well, that might be kind of tough right now, but when you get to heaven, ask him if he would do things differently the second time around.)*

 How do you think David's life would have been different had he decided to run from temptation instead of pursuing his lust for Bathsheba? Write your thoughts here.

JOSEPH was faced with some tough choices too. He chose to run from Potiphar's wife and it cost him some time in prison. Doesn't seem fair, but God honored Joseph for being obedient. He became the #2 man in charge in Egypt and he was a foreigner. Joseph's obedience eventually saved his own family from hardship and starvation. *(You can check this story out in Genesis 39-50.)*

 How do you think Joseph's story could have ended if he had decided to give in to Potiphar's wife? What might have been Joseph's legacy? Write your ideas here.

Both **DAVID** and **JOSEPH** were in a situation to sin against God. They each had a decision. Joseph decided that he would obey God and suffered imprisonment and then was blessed by God. David made the wrong choice and suffered the consequences. He did receive God's blessing after he confessed his sin and repented of it, but it cost him for the rest of his life. He did not get to see his dream of building the temple fulfilled because he decided to go against God's commands.

Two men. Two different decisions. TWO MEN LOVED BY GOD. *Two men who had* THE SAME OPPORTUNITY *to be obedient.*

What you do today will effect your
TOMORROW!

SESSION TWO:

Flirting With Temptation

Sarah clutched her stuffed bear, rocked back and forth, and sobbed uncontrollably. In between sobs she asked, "Why did this happen to me?" Her parents stood by, helpless and heartbroken, knowing the answer but unable to speak.

Sarah was 14 years old, but she felt as if her life was already over. Again and again, she retold the situation—Gary was very cute and much older. They met through mutual friends in the neighborhood, and she saw right away that he noticed her. How exciting it seemed—this 23-year-old "man" dropping by her house, flirting with her, and finally, asking her to sneak out of her bedroom window at night to meet him. At first she told him, "No way!" but the fantasy filled her mind day and night.

Sarah had become a Christian just two months earlier. She was working hard at her grades. She was attending church and felt she could handle Gary even though her mother had already warned her not to go near him. To Sarah, this new relationship seemed to fit into her desire to become a more mature person.

The first night she sneaked out was so exciting and romantic. Nothing really happened except for a some kissing and hand holding. Compared to what the other couples around them were doing, this seemed harmless to her. Sarah continued to slip out and go with Gary every chance she got. When they went to a party where everyone else was drinking, Sarah was proud of her ability to say no to the alcohol. Before long it was easy to tell her parents one thing, but end up with Gary and whatever his plan was for the evening. Sarah felt in control of life and bragged to her friends about how cool her new boyfriend was.

On this evening, though, Gary was different. He had already been drinking and was a bit rough in his kisses. He started driving recklessly and took Sarah to a deserted field where he announced, "It's time for you to follow through on your teasing and really grow up." That night Sarah became a victim of date rape and her fantasies turned into nightmares.

This is truly A DISASTER STORY.

In your opinion, how could Sarah have possibly avoided this entire nightmare?

Let's take a look at the process of temptation.

1. THE BATTLE for your body BEGINS IN THE MIND.

Girls fantasize about romance while boys dream about sex. Gary knew exactly what he wanted from Sarah, but she romanticized the relationship into something it was not. Be careful what plays on the small screen of your mind; it will be acted out on the big screen of life.

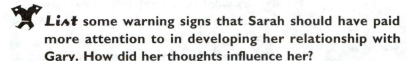 **List** some warning signs that Sarah should have paid more attention to in developing her relationship with Gary. How did her thoughts influence her?

David looked at Bathsheba taking a bath and the thought process was enough to topple a king described as *"a man after his [God's] own heart" (1 Sam. 13:14)*. If somebody greater than you and me falls by giving in to fantasy, then we can fall too. Don't watch movies with sexual themes or scenes; don't read books that stir up sexual feelings and ideas; choose carefully who you hang with.

 Do not give the devil a foothold (Eph 4:27).

2. LOOK BEYOND the glitter of TV AND MOVIES by asking God to CHANGE YOUR "WANT TO'S."

In *I John 1:9* we are told to *"confess our sins."* Literally, we are being asked to "agree with" God about our sin, to have the same feeling toward it as He does. Sarah allowed herself to compare her sinful behavior by what others were doing instead of God's Word. This way it didn't seem so bad. The casual references to sex on television sometimes leaves us thinking that illicit sexual behavior is "normal."

Do you compare what you do by what others are doing, or do you compare what you do by God's Word?

❑ *Others*

❑ *God's Word*

While we flirt and fantasize with sexual sin, God abhors it. He absolutely hates it! If we submit our hearts to Him and ask Him to make us see sin as He does, we'll be strong enough to run away from, rather than be drawn to, sexual sin.

Pray and ask God to help you see sin as He does and to help you keep your thoughts away from sin.

3. Don't be fooled—IT CAN HAPPEN TO ANYBODY.

Never let self-assurance blind you to the possibility of an attack. Sarah mistakenly believed she was above the temptation and could remain in control regardless of the circumstances around her.

Sarah was a Christian and attended church. What is one thing she could have done as a Christian to remind herself to make right decisions? How would it have helped her?

Check the items that Sarah could have done to help her from getting into this situation. Sarah could have...

☐ said "No Way!" and stood firm in her answer.

☐ obeyed her mother.

☐ honestly evaluated why a 23-year-old-man would be interested in dating a 14-year-old-girl.

☐ spent more time with her Christian friends.

☐ asked God to help her with the temptation she was facing and realized that God does not expect us to face temptation alone.

☐ read God's Word to see what direction it could give her about this type of temptation.

Peter was warned personally about his temptation to deny Jesus.

Peter declared, "Even if I have to die with you, I will never disown you." And all the other disciples said the same (Matt 26:35).

Peter DID deny Jesus—three times, even though earlier he declared that he would not. (See *Matt. 26:70,72,74.*) Just as Peter let self-assurance blind him to the possibility of an attack, Sarah let it blind her to the possibility of an attack. It can happen to anybody, it happened to Peter and Sarah. It can happen to you.

So if you **THINK YOU ARE STANDING FIRM, BE CAREFUL that you don't fall (1 Cor. 10:12).**

4. You've got to BELIEVE! You've got to CHOOSE.

God will give you the power to overcome temptation. When Sarah's mother warned her about Gary, God *was* providing Sarah with protection and escape from the temptation. If she had listened, she would have avoided great heartache.

God is faithful; he will not let you be tempted beyond what you can bear. But when you are tempted, he will also provide a way out so that you can stand up under it (1 Cor. 10:13).

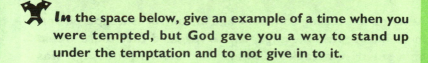

In the space below, give an example of a time when you were tempted, but God gave you a way to stand up under the temptation and to not give in to it.

5. GET ACCOUNTABLE.

Pray for a friend of the same sex who will hold you accountable for your actions and pray for you daily. This could be a fellow student, a Sunday School teacher, or a friend, but you must be committed to the promise.

 Two are better than one...IF ONE FALLS DOWN, HIS FRIEND CAN HELP him up (Eccl. 4:9).

Sarah's new church friends were obviously not part of her social life. She went on Sundays but hung out with a different crowd during the week. Share your temptations openly, pray about them together, and ask God for strength to move forward.

 Fill in the blank with the name of a Christian friend that will help you be accountable to God for your actions. Pray for your friend.

My friend _____ will pray for me and will encourage me to do what God teaches when I am faced with temptation.

America was feeling confident and in control as a superpower. In an intercepted message, it was revealed that there would be a surprise attack on Pearl Harbor. The message was marked "routine" rather than "urgent." The warning had been received, but it was ignored. Tragically the surprise attack happened and it began World War II.

Just like America ignored the message of the surprise attack, Sarah ignored all of the warnings in her relationship with

Gary. She felt confident and in control of the situation, but she was setting herself up for a surprise attack.

Many students set themselves up for a surprise attack in their dating relationships. They feel in control and ignore warning signs in the relationship. When the surprise attack suddenly comes, they simply aren't ready.

Be Ready for Battle

Tom

Tom was a strong Christian. In high school he had a few flings with alcohol, but he repented and was on the straight path. He left for college full of confidence and excitement about the future. Tom was active in student government and was an immediate social success. He went to parties but never drank and was respected for his stand. He bragged about being the designated driver and was not ashamed to tell everyone about his beliefs.

Tom kept going to parties where alcohol flowed and casual sexual acquaintances were "normal." Unfortunately one night of giving in to drinking a few beers destroyed the witness Tom had spent months building. He had a night of sex he could barely remember with a girl he didn't even know, shattering a two year relationship with a Christian girl he really cared for. The guys didn't miss Tom's actions, and bragged to each other that they had finally "won" the battle with Tom. Tom's spirit was crushed and he went into depression for weeks.

Do you think Tom was setting himself up for a surprise attack? Where did Tom begin to go wrong?

Tom was the victim of a surprise attack because he continued to walk the battlefield in a mode of "routine." The Bible warns us to set our guard in an "urgent mode."

 Be sober, be vigilant; because your adversary the devil, as a roaring lion, walketh about, seeking whom he may devour (1 Pet. 5:8).

Satan doesn't give up in his assaults and plans his attack on three areas: *The battle for the mind, the body, and the soul.*

1. THE MIND
There are many forces that can assault your mind. A few of these are:

• Alcohol and drugs
The command to be sober literally means "to build a wall of protection around" and "to have a mind free from intoxicants." Alcohol and drugs hurt the mind by causing lack of judgment and inability to think or care about con-

sequences. One look around the school campus and you can clearly see how alcohol and drugs break down the best of intentions.

Some FACTS about alcohol:

Fact: Alcohol-related accidents are the leading cause of death for people ages 16-24.[1]

Fact: According to one study, 90% of all rapes involving college students occurred when the victim or the attacker was under the influence of alcohol.[2]

Fact: Half of all 16-19 year olds were more likely to have sex if they and their partner had been drinking.[3]

Fact: The U.S. standard for legal intoxication is .10% of blood alcohol level, but research shows that brain functioning is impaired at .05%.[4]

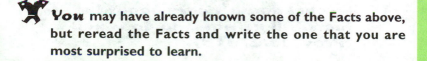 **You** may have already known some of the Facts above, but reread the Facts and write the one that you are most surprised to learn.

• Anger and hurt feelings

Allowing anger and hurt feelings to grow within you can have an overwhelming power over decisions. Lives have been ruined in an effort to "get even" or boost self-esteem. The Bible has a lot to say about anger and hurt feelings.

> An angry man stirs up dissension, and a hot-tempered one commits many sins (Prov. 29:22).

Only fools insist on quarreling...It is hard to stop a quarrel once it starts, so don't let it begin (Prov. 20:3b; 17:14, TLB).

> Sinners love to fight (Prov. 17: 19, TLB).

A fool gets into fights. His mouth is his undoing! His words endanger him (Prov. 18:6-7, TLB).

> A rebel doesn't care about the facts. All he wants to do is yell (Prov. 18:2, TLB).

More Scripture verses are in the Book of Proverbs about the consequences of anger, revenge, and holding grudges. For a right attitude, look up *Proverbs 19:11* and *20:3a* in your Bible and write them below.

• Sinful habits

Are you watching movies or reading materials that fill your mind with sexual ideas? That's like pouring gasoline on a fire. You become your own worst enemy. Confess these today with a full heart of repentance and deal with the nagging enemies once and for all.

Are you struggling with sinful habits? Ask God to help you cultivate the habit of protecting yourself from temptation in everyday life and to look at life with a clear heart and mind. Read *Luke 22:40*.

2. THE BODY

Be *vigilant* is translated "to be morally alert." This is more than saying no to sexual advances. It is carefully thinking through where to go on a date; who to go with; what type of message you give through your behavior, talk, the clothes you wear; and what situations to be in.

Virtue is defined as "moral excellence." How do you accomplish it? With great effort and intention. One well-known sports executive confided in me—"I have girls calling me, offering me sex constantly. As a Christian single, I have to daily confirm my moral goals to myself before the temptation comes. And, I run...a lot!" Stay physically active to keep your body's appetites under control. Direct your energies into projects and goals. This is a life characterized by the control of natural appetites and a commitment to the purpose of God.

On a separate sheet of paper, write a dating plan of "moral excellence." Include where you will go, the person you will go with, what you will say, do, wear, and think. Use this dating plan as your guide to guard against temptation.

3. THE SOUL

The enemy of our souls is, of course, the devil. This particular enemy is more dangerous than any army of soldiers because his attack is for all eternity. Peter emphatically stresses the urgency to *cast all your anxiety upon him* [God] *because he cares for you* (1 Pet. 5:7). If you have already experienced a surprise attack in your moral life, the experience of repentance and salvation is available to cleanse and heal you. In fact, the battle for your soul has already been fought and won when Christ died on the cross for your sins and was raised from death to sit at the right hand of God. Be sure today that you have received Christ as your personal Savior by committing your heart to Him and accepting the gift of His death on the cross. This can be done in five easy steps.

Step 1:   Admit that you are a sinner. *(Rom. 3:23)*
Step 2:   Believe that Jesus is God's Son who died for your sins, was buried, and then raised from the dead. *(Rom. 5:8)*

Step 3: Commit your life to Him by asking Him to be the Lord of your life. *(Rom. 10:9-10; Phil. 2:9-11)*

Step 4: Pray for salvation. *Dear God, I realize I am a sinner. I believe Jesus died for me on the cross and was raised from death to provide forgiveness and eternal life. Please save me as I turn from my sins to Jesus. Amen.*

Step 5: Now you must stand up in celebration of the victory by living for Him and doing the will of God. Tell someone about the choice you just made.

Jesus warned Peter, *"Satan has asked to sift you as wheat."* Satan also asked God for permission to test Job *(Job 1:6-12)*. Temptations, my friend, are everywhere, and we must set a guard for the mind, the body, and the soul. It is *eternally* dangerous to flirt with temptation.

DON'T PLAY GAMES WITH STUFF THAT PLAYS FOR KEEPS.

Ask God to help you on life's battlefield of temptation to always be ready for any surprise attacks and to have and follow a plan for moral excellence.

[1] Ziva Branstetter, "Students and Alcohol," Yo! Houston, Houston Chronicle, May 5, 1994. 5.

[2] Brenda Rios, "Soaring Alcohol Abuse Puts College Women at High Risk," Houston Chronicle, June 8, 1994. 5a.

[3] "When Students Use Alcohol, Look Behind the Bottle," USA Today and AP, April 14.

[4] "25 Years Ago: Driving Drunk," Popular Science, May 1994. 140.

SESSION THREE:

How Far Is Too Far on a Date?

If you worked through the first two sessions and are still wondering how far is too far, you need to go back to session one again. (As in Monopoly®, you passed GO! but you didn't collect your $200.) Students who experiment sexually and justify promiscuity are using the wrong standard to start with. Sure, you're keeping your clothes on , but your hands are running everywhere. Does that make it right? Or your clothes are off, but you're not actually engaging in intercourse. Aren't you "technically" still a virgin?

Whoa, right there! You've missed the whole point. Remember, when you make a stand for virtue, you are pursuing moral excellence, not moral "maybe."

 IT'S NOT WHAT YOU'RE DOING, IT'S WHO YOU'RE BECOMING.

The Brakes Don't Always Work

I'll never forget Rosemary from down the street. We were both 15, and I thought she was the finest thing ever! Whenever she came out of the house, I'd race my motorcycle to her driveway, slam on the brakes and spray gravel all over her. I did this about five times thinking surely she'd be impressed even though she was black and blue from the stones! One day my grand display of power backfired when the brakes failed. I gripped the bike and put all my energy into the brakes, but nothing happened. I skidded past Rosemary, through the next door neighbor's yard, and into the creek behind the house. Rosemary and the rest of the neighborhood had a great laugh as I pushed the motorcycle home, sloshing water and mud as I walked. I learned that day that in spite of good intentions, the brakes don't always work!

 Write about an embarrassing experience you've had when you were trying to impress someone.

Once you begin riding on the immoral fast lane, you just might find out your brakes can't act fast enough. You can rationalize that you aren't going as fast as some others, but you're still speeding and in danger of going out of control.

Girls and guys are different. Oh, you noticed! But in many ways other than just physical. Generally speaking, to a girl, intimacy involves hugging and snuggling, She loves to cuddle, to be held, and hear "sweet talk." Much of her sexual needs are fulfilled in this way. But for a guy, this same hugging and snuggling is anything but contentment. Instead it is a beginning that longs to be completed in a sexual act. This, of course, can pose a great dilemma. She is happy kissing for an hour; he thinks this hour is just a warm up!

Yes, keeping your sexual feelings under control is difficult, but it is not impossible! However, if you allow yourselves to constantly snack on appetizers, soon your appetite will be craving the whole enchilada! Don't get started making out when there is no possible way to please God.

How far is too far? Anything that stirs up sexual feelings in you that cannot be righteously fulfilled is too far.

Look at this chart from Josh McDowell found in the *True Love Waits Bible* (p 1105). Physical affection is a progressive process—one stage naturally leads to the next.

Abstinence
Holding Hands
Hugging
Casual Kissing

Prolonged Kissing
Light Petting
Heavy Petting
Intercourse

Let's go back to the beginning and think in the future tense. The goal is moral excellence. When you ask the question, "How far is too far?" you are really asking, "How far away can I stray without changing the goal?" Write your goal. See the goal with your heart. Now what should the question be?

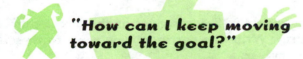

"How can I keep moving toward the goal?"

Experimenting sexually with or without clothing can only move you away from your pursuit of moral excellence. In fact, when you pursue an intimate relationship with God, the Holy Spirit within you will caution you strongly when immorality takes over the mind.

The goal is MORAL EXCELLENCE. To achieve the goal, begin at the end—to stay strong, **you have to WALK STRONG**.

1. DEVELOP A LIFE OF PRAYER. Prayer is communication with God, the author and perfector of our faith (*Heb. 12:2*). Talk with Him daily about your goals, your dreams, your hopes. Jesus gave us examples of prayer.

Read *John 17*. Jesus knew His strength came through prayer. He was wise enough to share His struggles in prayer. Identify these points in His talks with the Father:

Stated His goal _____

_____

Struggles in reaching the goal _____

_____

Discussion of events along the way _____

_____

Recommitment to truth _____

_____

Read *Matthew 6:9-13*, Jesus gives us the direct command to pray. Write the corresponding verse to these elements of prayer:

Praise—*Matthew 6:* _____

Commitment to God's will—*Matthew 6:* _____

Faith for God's provision—*Matthew 6:* _____

Forgiveness of sin—*Matthew 6:* _____

Power over temptation and the evil one—*Matthew 6:*

_____

Affirmation of truth—*Matthew 6:* _____

2. KNOW THAT GOD UNDERSTANDS WHAT YOU'RE GOING THROUGH. Remember that Jesus walked the earth as a man. He was a single man surrounded by popularity and rejection by family and friends. He definitely experienced temptation in the flesh and depression in the spirit. Don't ever think He is asking too much of you. Remind yourself that He left heaven and came to earth for the purpose of experiencing your pain and giving His life that you might live forever.

We do not have a high priest who is unable to sympathize with our weaknesses, but we have one who has been tempted in every way, just as we are —yet was without sin (Heb. 4:15).

"How can I find strength to overcome my inner struggles?" you ask. The answer to your question is found in *Hebrews 4:16*. Memorize it; use it daily.

Let us then approach the throne of grace with confidence, so that we may receive mercy and find grace to help us in our time of need (Heb. 4:16).

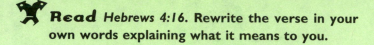 **Read** *Hebrews 4:16.* Rewrite the verse in your own words explaining what it means to you.

Reread *Hebrews 4:16.* Write the verse below. Now, practice until you can say the verse from memory.

3. BELIEVE THAT GOD IS ON YOUR SIDE.

Help is on the way. You can read God's promises throughout the Word. Now, decide. Do you believe them or not? Don't say you do, yet talk about helpless feelings to say no to sexual fantasies or actions. You can choose to be under the influence of the most powerful force on earth 24 hours a day. Think about the awesomeness of that! The Creator of the universe, the One who hung the moon, made the stars, and told the seas "Stop, you've gone far enough." This is your God who loves you and cheers for you.

Therefore He is able to save completely those who come to God through Him, because he always lives to intercede for them (Heb. 7:25).

Read *Hebrews 7:25*. In the list of characteristics below, check the characteristics of Christ that you see in *Hebrews 7:25*.

☐ **trustworthy**	☐ **eternal**
☐ **sincere**	☐ **able**
☐ **helpful**	☐ **consistent**
☐ **savior**	☐ **peacemaker**
☐ **patient**	☐ **caring**
☐ **righteous**	☐ **pure**

4. CHOOSE ONE STANDARD: GOD.

Decide today there will be no other standard for your pursuit of moral excellence. Society changes its moral code like fashion designers change styles—whatever the majority says is good. The human mind cannot produce an objective standard of truth and morality because it is influenced by individual experience, it changes, and it has a human time span. The real danger comes when we start to compare what we are tempted to do with what others are doing.

God's nature and character define truth. God is truth. Everything we call moral, every good thing is from God. The reason some things are right and some things are wrong is because there exists a Creator, Jehovah God, and He is a righteous God.

 God is the standard we need.

To what standard have you been comparing your behavior up until now?

☐ *my own ideas of right and wrong*
☐ *my parents and what they say*
☐ *my friends and what they say*
☐ *my teachers and what they say*
☐ *my society and what it says*
☐ *my church and what it says*
☐ *other* _____

Don't fall for the stuff being peddled in most sex ed. classes, on TV, or by your friends. They weaken the warning by saying, "You have to be emotionally ready for sex. Wait until you are older. It's OK as long as you are 'safe.'" Students can debate all day: "Am I ready? Am I old enough for sex?" Stop wondering. God doesn't beat around the bush. In fact, a misunderstanding is impossible:

> It is God's will...that you avoid sexual immorality; that each of you should learn to control his own body in a way that is holy and honorable (1 Thess. 4:3-4).

ANY QUESTIONS ON THAT ONE?

To what standard will you compare your behavior from now on?

❏ my own ideas of right and wrong

❏ my parents and what they say

❏ my friends and what they say

❏ my teachers and what they say

❏ my society and what it says

❏ my church and what it says

❏ God's standard

5. AIM FOR HOLINESS.

The word *holy* is found 600 times in different forms throughout the Bible. Do you think we should check it out?

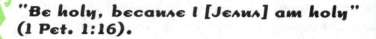

"Be holy, because I [Jesus] am holy" (1 Pet. 1:16).

Holiness is taken from the root word *hale*, meaning "wholeness, healthy, fulfilled." It is to be separated from sin and dedicated to God. This is truly God's plan for every life. We are told to *make every effort to...be holy (Heb. 12:14)* which means we need to seriously work at it.

How can we make every effort to develop holiness? The four steps toward holiness are:

1. Accept the challenge. Decide to train for holiness.

2. Know what is expected. Christians must know what is expected from holy lives that please God.

3. Obey the Instructor. Christians must follow God's instructions and directions.

4. Be a part of the team. Christians can bond and draw strength and help from other Christians in their search for holiness.

Who is our example? Jesus gave us many heroes and heroines in the Bible as well as stories of those who gave in to temptation. These can certainly offer wisdom and strength. We can pursue holiness because we have:

• The example of Christ: *Be imitators of God (Eph. 5:1).*

God is not asking us to do the impossible. He is asking us to respond to all that He is already doing in us and for us to help us be holy. He, the Father, is in us, His Son is in us, His Holy Spirit is in us—all working to make us more like God.

 God has given you everything He has, for everything you need so you can walk with Him and be like Him. How are you responding to Him and what He has provided for you?

• The promise of Christ working in us: *For it is God who works in you to will and to act according to His good purpose (Phil. 2:13).*

Holiness releases all He is into all we are, to bring us to all we can become, and all we can achieve. It's a choice, and it's a choice each of us makes. Will we believe Him?

It's a choice, and it's a personal choice. Will you believe Him?

☐ **yes**   ☐ **no**

- The Holy Spirit to guide us: *He will guide you into all truth (John 16:13).*

Holiness is not just a set of rules and regulations. It's not taking out of life everything that brings happiness and joy. It's not a lot of restrictions and limitations. Holiness is God's total fulfillment in the one life God gave each of us. Holiness ensures God's best for us. But, lack of holiness guarantees loss, brokenness, emptiness, pain, incompleteness, sorrow, darkness, and death.

- The power of God available to us: *Now to him who is able to do immeasurably more than all we ask or imagine, according to his power that is at work within us (Eph. 3:20).*

Write praises to God...

...for making His power available to us.

...for giving more than we ask.

...for doing more than we ask.

...for working within us.

- **The purpose of God:** *For he chose us in him before the creation of the world to be holy and blameless in his sight (Eph. 1:4).*

By God's grace we are enabled to adopt a lifestyle of holiness, that is, obedience to the will of God. With His help, by guarding our minds and emotions, controlling our appetites and desires, we develop holy habits that will remain with us as we grow.

Habits affect character, and character affects the choices you make, and the choices you make will determine the shape and direction and outcome of your life. Holy habits of prayer, Bible study, and worship are essential in a life of holiness.

What habits are you creating in your life? Are they leading you toward your goal of moral excellence?

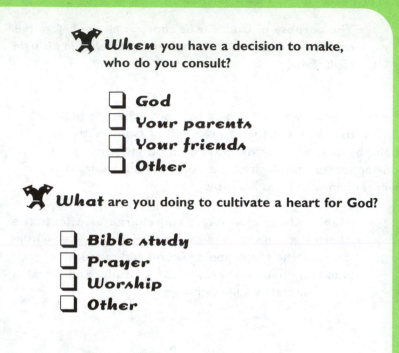

When you have a decision to make, who do you consult?

- ☐ God
- ☐ Your parents
- ☐ Your friends
- ☐ Other

What are you doing to cultivate a heart for God?

- ☐ Bible study
- ☐ Prayer
- ☐ Worship
- ☐ Other

When you choose to live your life in vital relationship with God in Jesus Christ, (a holy life) *you can experience no limit to what God can do through you.*

SESSION FOUR:

"Is Sex Wrong if You're Really in Love?"

"Is sex wrong if you're really in love?" (Enquiring minds want to know.) That's a question I get asked often. Most people when they ask it say, "But we are really in love. We're committed. This is true love. Surely this is different. I mean, I couldn't even begin to put into words how our love is."

RATIONALIZATION FACTOR

Ah, yes, the Rationalization Factor. *The American Heritage Dictionary* defines *rationalize* as "to devise self-satisfying but incorrect reasons for one's behavior." Contemporary language would say, "I do what I want because it is really what I want to do. I will find a way to explain it."

The greatest example is when Satan asked Eve if she was sure of what God said. Maybe He really did not mean what He actually said. After all, maybe she misunderstood or God was mistaken.

She took this new information, weighed it against God's instruction, and decided God was trying to cramp her style. She rationalized that this fruit would benefit her and therefore it was a good thing for her, not a bad thing. She learned the hard way that God's instruction was to save her life not ruin it. (See *Gen. 2:16–3:7.*) (Now before you jump Eve's case, given the same set of circumstances, you would have probably done the same thing. Most of us do it everyday. We try to outsmart God with the decisions in our lives.)

Whether constructing a building or our lives, the first step is always the same—lay a solid foundation. Our foundation is not a thing, but a person, and His name is Jesus.

No one can lay any foundation other than the one already laid, which is Jesus Christ (1 Cor. 3:11).

Take a look at *Matthew 7:24-28.* You know the story. Jesus compared those who heard Him and obeyed with those who heard Him and decided to do it their own way. See if you can match up the foolish and wise characteristics. Put a (F) for foolish and (W) for wise beside the correct description.

_____ Does what Jesus said was right to do.

_____ Seems to think sand is a good foundation.

_____ Hears the words of Christ and disobeys.

_____ Builds his life upon the rock of God.

Pretty easy exercise, but it seems that this one is easy on paper, but we fail miserably when it comes to applying this to our lives. Stop building on the sand and build your life on the rock.

Sexual purity can only be determined by God's standard. So many students stand strong in many areas, but allow the area of sexuality to be their downfall. The winds howl, the floods come, and our moral houses crash. We are left devastated and lonely.

 Review God's standard for sexual immorality that you learned in **Session Three, page 42.** Write God's standard below.

Remember, we are to be holy, because our foundation, Jesus Christ, is holy. Now that we've got the foundation secure, let's talk about some practical issues. Many psychologists believe that the average female student falls in and out of love at least 10 times. The male student falls in and out of love about half as many times. Obviously, if you give yourself sexually to everyone you are "in love" with, you will be sexually and emotionally scarred, as well as spiritually bankrupted. As a result, the possibility of a fulfilling rela-

tionship with the mate God has chosen for you be-
comes less.

A STEP FURTHER

Go a step further. Now you're engaged, or at least thinking about it. Things are serious and you know for sure
this is "the one." Now you're wondering—it's going to be
just us two forever, why wait any longer? Surely God
knows this is different. You can be sure He does know.
Remember, God sees the future the way we see yester-
day. God's intention is that you enjoy the gift of sexual intimacy; in fact, He is the creator of it. He asks that you
wait until marriage. Why would He do such a thing? Who
does He think He is? God! That's exactly
who He is. And it is in our best interest not to forget it!

Take a look at three stories where they decided to take
things into their own hands.

MARIANNE

Marianne grew up in the church where her dad was the
pastor. She was in college before seriously dating, and
now was engaged to Jeff, a wonderful Christian guy.
Both had the same goals and dreams, both were committed to full-time Christian service. They stayed
morally pure by mutual consent, but things started to
heat up a bit after he gave her the engagement ring.
They counted down the months to graduation and marriage and soon found themselves going farther and farther physically. They discussed it and decided this was
natural since they were engaged and soon began having
occasional sexual intercourse. Marianne got pregnant
with five months left before the wedding. She cried as
she thought how disappointed her parents would be,
but reasoned she and Jeff could move up the wedding

date to avoid total embarrassment. Imagine how she felt when Jeff said he had begun having second thoughts a few months ago and didn't think it was a good idea to get married after all.

JASON

Jessica and Jason had been dating for two months. Jason realized he was falling in love with Jessica. She was a Christian. She was active in her church. Jessica talked often to Jason about the Lord and how much she wanted to live a holy life. She told Jason about signing a *True Love Waits* commitment card at a rally last year. Jessica had made it clear that when she married she would only marry someone that was also committed to being sexually abstinent until marriage. Jason didn't know how to tell Jessica that he already suffered from a sexually transmitted disease because of an earlier mistake. And he wasn't sure he was as totally committed to being sexually abstinent as Jessica was. Jason knew that once he told Jessica of his earlier sexual activity she would never consider marrying him. He wished he had made a commitment to be sexually abstinent. Jason wished he had met Jessica earlier in his life. He was sorry that he couldn't erase the past and that he would have to live with the consequences of his choices.

LINDA

I noticed Linda's engagement ring and her obviously pregnant shape when she came to talk to me. She cried as she explained—"Don and I were so in love. My parents loved him; he was everything I ever dreamed about and prayed for. I was glad I had waited to give myself to this one man. As we counted down the days to the wedding, we began to feel married. Buying our rings, setting up the apartment, and planning for the future all solid-

ified our intentions. That's why when we slept together that night it didn't seem wrong. A few days later Don
was killed in a car accident. He never knew that I was
pregnant, and my child will never know his daddy.
Please share my story with other students. I hope it will
save them the pain and shame I live with."

Are you thinking, *Those are tragic stories, but we're going
to use birth control*. There it is. Rationalization, again!
The bottom line is—*you don't know what tomorrow
holds*. Only God does. He says wait, please! OK, you
know what He says, but why does He say it? You can be
sure the Creator has a good reason.

Pick one of the stories about Marianne, Jason, or
Linda. Rewrite it using God's standard for the individu-
als in the story.

Sexual intercourse provides a level of intimacy that cannot
be compared. It is a gift created by God for your enjoyment.
But because it is such a powerful pleasure, it can easily over-
take the other areas of your relationship. This intense intimacy can be mistaken for love and stifle growth in a couple.
Many couples look back in marriage and see that they never
really got along great in between the sexual encounters before marriage. They didn't really know the little things and
habits about each other. They had become so distracted
physically that they never introduced themselves emotionally or spiritually. God has a perfect plan and purpose for
every area of our lives.

God has a plan and purpose for you—even on your dates. Stop sexual temptation from taking over by planning activities before you ever leave on the date. Let's practice doing that now. Use this time to plan a date.

Set personal limits: (Ask God to help you remember your commitment to sexual purity. Let your date know of your commitment.)

"I commit to sexual abstinence from this day until I enter a biblical marriage relationship."
Signed_____

Set time: (Set a time to start the date and a time to finish the date. Don't allow too much time alone—either in a car or at someone's house.)
Time: From: _____ To: _____

Plan activity: (go out to dinner; movie; miniature golf; skating; mall; student group activity)
Activity selected: _____

Consider a double or group date with Christian friends:
Names of friends: _____

The Theft

I'm reminded of a trip to that my family made with me to Romania. My little girl brought a beautiful blue satin nightgown to give as a gift to whoever the Lord led her to that night. She sat in the stadium bleachers talking with people, taking in the sights, and excited about the service. One little girl plopped down beside her and stayed very close. She thought, *This is the one, isn't she, Lord? She's the one I am to give the gown to.* Just then, something odd happened. The little girl spotted the gown in our bag and tried to steal it! Can you imagine? She was trying to steal what was intended to be freely and graciously given.

The Gift

So many well-meaning couples end up stealing sexual pleasure instead of waiting to enjoy this wonderfully created gift. God's intention is that you present yourselves to one another on your wedding night as a special, pure gift of love. From there you will grow together, explore together, and experience the fullness of His creation together. Are you willing to trust in God's way rather than your own?

If you have committed eternity to Christ through salvation, then you must commit each day to Him. If you are expecting Him to bless you with a wonderful future, then you must be willing to live God's way today.

My steps have held to your paths; my feet have not slipped (Ps. 17:5).

Have you ever received a gift, but before you could open it, someone told you the contents of the gift in detail, spoiling your surprise? How did it make you feel? Were you disappointed? Were you less interested in it? Were you less excited about it? Why?

Read *Psalm 37* below. When you commit to sexual abstinence, you are allowing God's Word to become real in your life. This decision is truly an act of faith in God's Word and should be sealed in prayer. This psalm gives instruction and tells of the gift God promises as a result of obedience to Him. (If you are in a relationship, read *Ps. 37* together as you discuss your decision for sexual purity. Pray together.)

Trust in the Lord, and do good; dwell in the land, and enjoy safe pasture. Delight yourself in the Lord and he will give you the desires of your heart. Commit your way to the Lord; trust in him and he will do this (Ps. 37:1-5).

 Be still before the Lord and wait patiently for him (Ps. 37:7).

Read the verses; talk about them; and seal your commitment to God and to each other in prayer. This gift of patience and waiting may seem senseless to others, but presented to God it is a precious offering. If you are dating, be sure both of you are participating in this commitment. It takes two, baby! The decision must be made together.

Too many times, we focus our energy in a dating relationship on what we can't do, instead of what we can do. Be creative with activities you can do.

Activities

Exercise: Walk, run, do aerobics, ride bicycles, lift weights, get outside and go crazy. Burn off some sexual tension.

Volunteer: Paint houses for the disabled or elderly. Feed the homeless. Become involved in providing meals for the elderly. Baby sit for single moms. Direct some of that intense love to others.

Plan Group Fun: Group dates can be lots of fun and take pressure off of you and the other couples involved. Think about it—other couples are probably experiencing the same struggles.

Attend Conferences and Concerts Together: You'll come out with positive images and grow together emotionally, mentally, and spiritually.

Take a Class: Learn a craft, a language, or a new computer program.

Start a Hobby: Build and fly kites together. Take up painting, co-ed sports team, or ceramics. This gives you an outlet for creative energy.

Study the Bible together: Grow in your faith and commitment to Christ. Do this in an area that is open and accessible to others. Some Bible studies have become sessions on the study of God's creation and I am not talking trees and grass here. Keep your eyes on the Creator and not His human creation during these Bible studies.

 You have been presented with several activities. List others that you would like to add:

Two are better than one, because they have a good return for their work: If one falls down, his friend can help him up. But pity the man who falls and has no one to help him up (Eccl. 4:9,10).

Stay involved in what God is doing in your relationship, family, church, and community. Maintaining a proper perspective of Him being involved in our relationships will deliver us from much harm and frustration.

Remember, it is not wrong to be tempted. It is sin however, to give in to the temptation that comes our way.

Take a look at *James 1:13-15* in your Bible. There is a great warning there. See the progression that temptation takes. Fill in the blanks.

When tempted, no one should say, "_____ is tempting me." For God cannot be _____ by evil, nor does he _____ anyone; but each _____ is tempted when, by his _____ evil desire, he is dragged away and enticed. Then, after desire has conceived, it gives _____ to _____; and sin, when it is full-grown, gives birth to _____.

His plan is perfect and His warnings are true. He wants the best for us and is our biggest fan.

Sexual purity—IT BEGINS IN THE HEART AND OVERTAKES THE MIND.

Sex: Isn't Everybody Doing It?

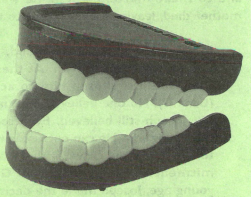

Don't believe the lie—all students are not doing it! The media sometimes gives the impression that virgins are an abnormal minority. Well, the truth is that not all students have fallen into the sexual trap. Many virgins are even happy to tell you it is by their own choice. The voice sometimes seems small, I'll agree, but one that is growing louder all the time. Much of the success of the moral revolution is due to the True Love Waits emphasis and to the public testimonies of students.

One such teen was Joseph, the youngest son of Jacob. Though his story is thousands of years old, it is as current as today's newspaper. The following is adapted from *The True Love Waits Bible* and is used by permission. Interwoven in the story's application are pearls of wisdom from students and young couples whose decision has been to wait until marriage. Together these make a powerful advocate for moral purity.

Like many of today's families, Joseph's was less than perfect. When he was 12, his mother died. He had a blended family of one father, several mothers, brothers, and sisters, and half-brothers and half-sisters. Sounds like many of the families I meet across the country! Jealousy, conflict, hatred, lust, rape, and deceit were woven through the family's history, yet God called Joseph to overcome temptation and stand tall in his faith. At first glance it appears as though the odds were stacked against Joseph—his brothers hated him, and to make matters worse, he was the baby. His mother died, leaving a busy father to take up for him.

In spite of a difficult childhood, Joseph grew up with a dream worth believing in. At the age of 17, he dreamed that God had chosen him to accomplish great things (*Gen. 37*). No one believed him, no one encouraged him, but Joseph still believed. Even today, God is looking for the young who He can entrust with dreams and motivate to rise above the crowd with a standard of absolute commitment to the principles of God's Word. At a very young age, Joseph made the decision to wait for a future of hope even though the present was full of despair.

MAKE YOUR DECISION AT AN EARLY AGE—*Deanna Hunt Carswell*

When I was about 14 years old, my Dad had a special ring made for me as a reminder to keep myself pure for my future husband. I accepted the gift and with an innocent heart embraced the principle. It stayed on my finger as a symbol and reminder of my decision until the day it was replaced by one from my husband, Jake. From the beginning of our relationship, purity was not a major obstacle because we had both made commitments to God as young students to remain pure until marriage. Everyone has struggles, but together we focused on God and what was His best for us.

- **Make your decision EARLY;**
- **Date a person who has also made this decision;**
- **MAKE IT AN ABSOLUTE for your life.**

It is your wedding night. You want to be honest with your new spouse and you begin recounting the details of your early dating life. Begin thinking now about what you want to be able to say. Write a paragraph "presenting" yourself to your future spouse.

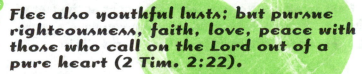

Flee also youthful lusts; but pursue righteousness, faith, love, peace with those who call on the Lord out of a pure heart (2 Tim. 2:22).

Joseph was also a young man of dedication. *Genesis 39:6* says Joseph was *well-built and handsome*. Naturally, women were attracted to him, including those with less than honorable intentions. Finding himself in a strange country and without family, he watched as those around him lived in sexual immorality.

DON'T GIVE SATAN A CHANCE
—Heath Thomas

As students, sexual purity is a driving force in our lives. When everything in our bodies, the world around us (advertisements, TV programs, the entertainment industry in general) and our peers emphasize the acceptance of sexual impurity, we are left in a tough position. In our personal spiritual lives, sexual purity stands as a stronghold that we cannot allow the enemy to breach. If we let down our guard and give in to impure actions, conversations or thoughts, we open the gates to the stronghold and imply surrender of God's best for a passing thrill.

Every student must set purity up as a crown to be fought for and protected to the glory of God. If you want to stay pure, don't prepare a date for impure actions. Time alone in a car to "talk" isn't realistic. As a student, our hormones are kicking like Bruce Lee. Satan wants to exploit that fact and cause us as warriors to fall and our purity to be taken. Think about the situations you put yourself in.

Get out of bad relationships. It doesn't matter how attractive the other person is—impurity is not a godly option. **Don't lay the crown of purity down at the feet of Satan** when it belongs at the feet of Jesus. Purity can only be attained when you have a growing, alive, meaningful relationship with Jesus Christ.

When Potiphar's wife tempted him with an offer of a one-night stand, no strings attached, Joseph didn't stop to think about it – he ran from this beautiful, evil, woman.

Jesus understands the temptations we endure even as He understood those Simon Peter would face. *"Simon, Simon, Satan* has asked to sift you as wheat. But I have prayed for you, Simon, that your faith may not fail" (Luke 22:31).

 Picture this: Jesus is kneeling today in prayer for you that your *"faith may not fail."* Can you see Him? Today is your day to issue an invitation—either Satan is allowed to step over the threshold into your decision-making or Jesus is offered free reign in your heart. Write your invitation below:

 Clothe yourselves with the Lord Jesus Christ and do not think about how to gratify the desires of the sinful nature (Rom. 13:14).

Joseph's boss' wife tempted him with sexual advances promising, "No one will know." It would have been easy for Joseph to give in to sin. Nevertheless, he held fast to the dream of a pure and holy life and the blessings of God. He asked, *"How then could I do such a wicked thing and sin against God?" (Gen. 39:9.)* Joseph did not submit to sin. He was wise enough to know that his sin would have been against God regardless if anyone else would have known. He chose to be obedient to God and God's plan for his future. We have the ability through Christ to make the same choice.

Live a Life of NO REGRETS!
There is no such thing as "secret sex." It will catch up with you as you live a double life. Spending years in church doing the right thing but for the wrong reasons—saying one thing, but doing another—brings a future of

emptiness. At least four people are directly hurt if you decide to have premarital sex: you and your future mate, your sexual partner and their future mate. How can you compare momentary happiness with a lifetime bond of marriage? The early adult years are meant for us to spend finding that one compatible person God specifically made for us. Think about the future blessing awaiting you and live a life of **NO REGRETS!** Don't just do it! Just wait!

- *live every day without regrets;*
- *don't just go through the motions of being a Christian—mean it, live it.*

Joseph had already made the decision before he was confronted with the temptation. When she told him "No one will know," he replied, "How could I do this sin against God?" He thought it through—yes, almost everybody else was doing it; true, no one else would know. None of that had any power against the future tense thinking. He was dedicated to the principles of God and the future obedience in them would bring. What about your future? Do you really, really believe God has the best planned for you—a future worth waiting for?

 Above all else, guard your heart, for it is the wellspring of life (Prov. 4:23).

Joseph was a teenager of great devotion. Four times *Genesis 39* recorded, *The Lord was with Joseph.* Make no mistake about it: What you are in secret will ultimately define you publicly. While Joseph's brothers partied and planned their evil, Joseph was praying; and God was preparing *"a hope and a future"* (Jer. 29:11). Because of Joseph's devotion, God sent a caravan to rescue him when his brothers had left him for dead. When thrown unjustly into prison, he received God's grace and wisdom.

The poverty of prison was replaced with the riches of position as Joseph became Prime Minister of Egypt. Joseph's greatness did not suddenly appear with adulthood. It grew out of his daily decisions to live for God and listen to God.

"For I know the plans I have for you," declares the Lord, "plans to prosper you and not to harm you, plans to give you hope and a future" (Jer. 29:11).

 Just imagine...what is God planning for your future? Who is He preparing to be your spouse? Since God created the universe, don't you think He can create your future? In your dating life, can you say as Joseph did "The Lord is with me"?

 Yes   No

One young couple in the Old Testament is a great example of purity. Check out Rebekah and Isaac. In *Genesis 24*, we see Abraham carefully choose the type of wife he wanted for his son, Isaac.

Her family and spiritual background were the most important criteria (vv. 1-4). As the servant was praying for God's best choice, a young woman came out: The girl was very beautiful, a virgin; no man had ever lain with her (v. 16). This seems like a lot of trouble just to find a wife, but it shows us the importance of waiting on God's best. Many dating possibilities will confront you, but don't go any further until you have God's blessings.

Abraham very carefully thought out the criteria for Isaac's wife. Make a list of what you want in a spouse. Pray over it and review it often over the years. You may revise it as your own personal goals change, but always keep it consistent with Scripture, and remind yourself to wait on the Lord's best even if it means breaking off a fun relationship.

SET GODLY, POSITIVE PATTERN IN YOUR LIFE—Brandon Thomas

True respect for your girlfriend will instill a desire to honor her and her commitments to the Lord. Accept her as an authentic individual and be authentic yourself. Look for God's best in a dating relationship and accept nothing less.

If there has been a mistake in the past, accept God's forgiveness and Move On! The best deterrent for the same mistake is to see how sin honestly grieves a woman of God and how it negatively affects the relationship. If the two of you cannot put the sin behind you and move on to purity in the relationship, it's time to get out of that relationship. Be willing to be honest, but understand the beauty of forgiveness and walk in the confidence of God's grace.

- **Respect yourself and your partner.**
- **Put the past behind and walk confidently in Christ.**
- **Accept nothing less than God's best.**

I beseech you therefore, brethren, by the mercies of God, that you present your bodies a living sacrifice, holy, acceptable to God, which is your reasonable service (Rom. 12:1).

Isaac went out to the field one evening to meditate, and as he looked up, he saw camels approaching (Gen. 24:63). Interesting that the one God had selected for him would come during a time of prayer. (It was the girl riding on the camel, not the camel God had prepared for Isaac. Just wanted to make that clear.)

Pray at the End of Each Date—Jason and Amy Breland

Jason and Amy

Jason and Amy Breland had prayed since childhood for God's best in a mate.

Amy and I met at college, and I was immediately attracted to her. She, however, was cautious. I asked her out several times before she accepted. In the meantime, we investigated each other's past and personalities by talking with mutual friends. I learned she had a reputation as a godly young woman of purpose which only made me want to know her more. We both made the commitment to moral purity long before the temptation to compromise could come along. We owe a great deal to our parents who taught us from the beginning that sex outside of marriage is sin.

Amy and I had committed to save ourselves for each other long before we knew each other. Because we were older and on our own, we were very careful not to be alone for long periods of time and ended every date with prayer. Knowing this habit of praying together was waiting for us gave a great deal of strength and put things in proper perspective for us. It also purified our decisions during the date about where to go and what to do.

 What does prayer have to do with dating and finding your future mate?

The servant then proceeded to tell Isaac all he had done and probably the instruction of his father. Isaac immediately set out to act appropriately and chose to marry Rebekah *(v. 66-67)*. Perhaps you are becoming serious about your dating partner and feel it is time to establish serious commitment. Read what one young man chose to do...

 ## A PROMISE IS A PROMISE—
Rafael Luciano

When my commitment had matured enough that I was ready to quit playing games, I chose to give my girlfriend a promise ring. This symbolized a serious friendship, a friendship for life. Along with that came the question of making sure that our temples were holy. What I wanted to do was give her a ring that would symbolize both a spiritual and physical commitment. Whatever we do as a couple must honor God.

> I told her that my love for her could only be as strong as my love for God; and if I didn't love Jesus first, I couldn't be committed to her. I promised from this day forward to be honest in everything I did and asked her to help me be committed to what we both agreed on—to stay pure, and to stay spiritually strong.

I described our relationship like a triangle—we're at opposite angle points heading toward the same goal point and we can only grow closer. Walking the same road hand in hand, we cannot be selfish in any area, including moral purity.

> The result of waiting on God's best for your mate is seen in the last part of *Genesis 24:67* when Isaac married Rebekah, *So she became his wife, and he loved her; and Isaac was comforted after his mother's death.* God's mate for you will bring joy, comfort, and mutual love to your life. Here is one last story about a young lady who has chosen to remain morally pure, especially as she looks toward the future.

DON'T TEMPT YOURSELF!—
Chris Strack

My parents have talked to me about moral purity since I was just a tiny girl. We prayed about being in God's will, and they passed on an excitement to me about trusting God with my future. Now, my boyfriend of two years and I share the same goal of absolute purity, and this is a great strength in our relationship. At the very beginning, we asked each other about what we believed and how we planned to behave. Setting a goal together of moral purity helps to take the pressure off and keeps us thinking in the future tense. We don't feel like we're giving up or missing anything. Instead, we look forward to God's best for our lives. Together, we set these rules for ourselves:

- **Don't be alone in a house together.**
- **Plan our dates before we go out.**

We both made the commitment to moral purity long before the temptation to compromise could come along.

> Don't modify your goals. Find someone who will happily join you in them. I volunteer at a local pregnancy center and have seen firsthand the devastation that unplanned pregnancy can cause. When a girl tells me she didn't mean to have sex but she is just so in love, I usually find that her boyfriend does not share a mutual goal of moral purity. Think about it—you can only fight and say no for so long. Don't put yourself in that position by dating anyone who doesn't stand strong for Christ and His principles. When a guy says, "If you love me, show me," don't be afraid to turn the tables—take him home and draw him a picture!

Whatever you do, whether in word or deed, do it all in the name of the Lord Jesus giving thanks to God the Father through him (Col. 3:17).

The bottom line—walk by faith, not by sight, not by feelings. Allow God to be vibrantly alive in your life; choose to walk in His ways; and to WAIT on His best.

Guidance

These Group Learning Activities are as easy as 1, 2, 3! Three divisions will help you in preparation and implementation of each session's activities. Each student needs a book because the activities refer them back into the books.

1—"Stuff You Need to Do," includes any special instructions for how to set up your meeting room; signs and banners you or your creative youth need to make; what to do with the supplies you have gathered, and any other suggestions to help your session go smoothly. Stuff You Need to Do will help you know the amount of advance preparation needed.

2—Next is the "Stuff You Need to Get." It is a good idea to always have extra Bibles on hand in your meeting room, as well as pencils, markers, construction paper, banner paper, current Christian artist cassettes or CDs, and a cassette or CD player. Some supplies listed may be optional. If you do not have access to every supply, be creative and come up with a substitution that would also work as well.

3—The third part of the guidance for each session is what to do "During the Session." Each session is designed to last 60 minutes. A suggested amount of time to spend on each activity is given; however, your group activity times may vary depending on the interest, speed, and size of your group. You will need to adjust the times within the 60 minutes for your specific needs. The activities suggest how to proceed with the group session with suggestions for what the leader should say in bold type.

Careful and deliberate preparation ensures your group sessions to be successful! Youth can always tell if a leader is prepared. Right now, thank God for the opportunity He has given you in leading this study on sexual purity. Ask Him to guide your preparations, words, and actions during this study and for Him to prepare the hearts and minds of the youth you will be leading.

SESSION ONE: THINK IN THE FUTURE TENSE

Stuff You Need to Do:

Tape down a large sheet of newsprint on the floor of the room you are meeting in. (Optional: If your meeting room is close to a sidewalk, use it with sidewalk chalk instead.) Use two pieces of poster board and label them across the top: (1) "When I was 5, I wanted to be a _____ when I grew up." (2) "When I was 10, I wanted to be a _____ when I grew up."

One way to get artistic youth involved in the study is by recruiting them ahead of time to create posters of some of the sayings in the text. These could be computer-created banners, hand-drawn posters, collages...whatever! A couple of phrases for this session might be: "It's time to BEGIN TODAY by thinking about TOMORROW'S END RESULT" and "What you do today will effect your tomorrow."

Stuff You Need to Get:

- **one** large piece of newsprint (big enough for a youth to lay down on); or,
- **six** different colors of sidewalk chalk
- **two** pieces of poster board

- **assorted** colors of markers
- **pencils**
- **extra** Bibles
- **cassettes** or CDs with songs about sexual purity and holiness

During the Session:

What Do You Want to Be When You Grow Up?

(15 minutes) As youth arrive for the study, encourage them to respond to the questions on the graffiti posters with the markers provided. During this time, play songs that relate to sexual purity and holiness.

To begin, have each youth share some of their answers from the posters. Share your own answers as well. (In fact, this is a good time to note that your honesty in sharing your life and especially your personal struggles and/or victories with sexual purity will be an important part of your leadership of this study. You don't have to go into sordid detail. The stories in this book provide excellent examples of honestly telling stories of sexual temptation without becoming a stumbling block.) **Say: Now, I'd like you to share what your "real" dreams are.** Give the youth three minutes to fill out questions 2, 3, and 4 from pages 8 and 9. **Say: Everything we're going to talk about for the next few sessions is based on your hopes and dreams. When you wrote down steps you needed to accomplish your goals, you probably didn't include "get pregnant" or "catch a sexually transmitted disease" or "ruin my reputation." But each of those things (and a whole lot of other stuff) is possible if you decide to be sexually active. And those kinds of things can block you from reaching your dreams.**

The Turning Point (20 minutes)

Ask the youth to fill out the checklist on page 16. Have them write in any goals that don't appear on the checklist. Split them into pairs and have them share the results of their checklist with each other. **Say: You may not be interested in all of these choices (I sure hope not!) In fact, you may not be interested in any of them. But you have to remember that each choice you make today...hey, each choice I make today affects what choices I can make tomorrow. A simple example is the choice of whether or not to go to college. For certain occupations** (you could have youth name some here), **a college education is a requirement. If you choose not to go, you are choosing not to get into those areas of employment. In the same way, what you choose to do or not to do sexually will open up or limit your choices down the line. Let's look at some of the choices a couple of Bible guys made in these areas.**

Assign each partnership either to the David and Bathsheba story (p. 18 and *2 Sam. 11*), or the Joseph and Potiphar's wife story (p. 18-19 and *Gen. 39*). Have them respond to the question in the book and be prepared to share their answers with the group. Give them five minutes to get ready.

As the partnerships share, have each group share one thing they think might have happened if David or Joseph had made different choices.

The Scene of the Crime (20 minutes)

Have one of the youth read the first paragraph of John and Heidi's story on page 11. Ask for volunteers to respond to the question that follows. After two or three people respond, have another youth continue reading the story. **Say: What a mess...and it didn't have to be** that way. We're going to use John and Heidi's story to think through five guidelines for dating wisely. In fact, we'll look at their story just like a detective looks at a crime scene. Have one of the youth lay down on the sidewalk or newsprint and draw an outline around them. Write the youth responses inside the outline of the body as you continue this discussion.

Use the material on pages 13-17 as background for a discussion of the five questions.

- *Who* is this person? What are their beliefs about moral purity? Are we moving toward the same goals in life? Ask the youth if they feel like John and Heidi had the same goals. Remind youth that just because someone asks you out does not mean you have to go out. (Extra credit crime scene question: Is John or Heidi the victim? The answer: Both of them are victims. They're missing out on the wonderful way God designed sexuality for marriage.)

- *Why* am I interested in dating him or her? Did the relationship begin as a friendship or a physical attraction? Ask youth about John's attraction to Heidi...friendship or physical? Also, note that this is the motive part of the crime.

  - *Where* will you go on dates? Are your interests and friends compatible? This is the scene of the crime. Ask youth if there are some places or situations that might make doing something stupid sexually easier.

- *What* can I expect as a result of this relationship? How will I be challenged and changed by this person's influence on me? When you date someone, you will become more like them. For example, I became a fan of Broadway musicals and The Beatles, because that was what my girlfriend was into. Would you want to become more like this person?

- **Will** this choice honor my parents and God? Will it strengthen my goals and motivate me to stay on track? We're back where we started...with goals and dreams? Suggest to the youth that one of the best questions they could ask is "Could I ask God to bless (and/or honor) this relationship?" If the answer is "NO," then it's time to bail out of the relationship.

An extra credit assignment: have one or more of your youth who are good with computers to make up a "5 W's" card with the questions on it. Have them pass it out to the class next week.

Closing (5 minutes)

To close, stand around the body outline and hold hands. Lead in prayer, asking that God would help the youth to think ahead in their sexual decisions and that He would help them to think wisely through their dating practices.

SESSION TWO: FLIRTING WITH TEMPTATION

Stuff You Need to Do:

Prepare three, three-by-five-inch cards with assignments on them as follows.

- **Read** the section entitled "Alcohol and Drugs," pages 28-29. Then answer the statement at the end of the section. Be prepared to share some of your answers with the group.

- **Read** the section entitled "Anger and Hurt Feelings," pages 30. Then answer the question at the end of the section. Be prepared to share the two proverbs that meant the most to your group with the rest of your group.

- **Read** the section entitled "Sinful Habits," page 31. Read *Luke 22:40* and *Psalm 101:3*. Pick out three **TV** shows that youth commonly watch that would easily become sinful habits. Be prepared to share your answers with the group.

> Set the room up dividing it in half with chairs with a wall equal distance behind each side.

Enlist a youth to give a short (3-4 minutes) testimony on how he/she came to Jesus. Make sure you meet with this youth before the session to check over what they are going to say.

> Once again, get artistic youth involved by recruiting them ahead of time to create posters of some of the sayings in the text. A couple of phrases for this session might be:

> "Don't play games with stuff that plays for keeps" and "The battle for your body begins in your mind."

Stuff You Need to Get:

- **three** three-by-five-inch cards
- **two** sheets of paper for every person attending half of the sheets one color, the other half another color
- **pencils**
- **extra** Bibles
- **optional:** TV and VCR

During the Session:

It's a Battle (10 minutes)

Hand each youth two pieces of paper and have them crumple the paper into paper wads. Divide the group into two teams (the easiest way to do this is by the color of paper you hand out to them). Assign each team one wall of the room you are meeting in and divide the room down the middle with chairs. Each team must stay on its side of the chairs. The object of the game is to hit the opposing team's wall with your paper wads. Team members may block the paper wads with their bodies and pick wads up from the floor on their side of the chairs. Have someone at each wall counting the number of hits (this is a fast and furious game). The winner is the first team to score 20 hits. Play this game two or three times.

Say: This has just been a battle with paper wads...but each of us face a battle with temptation on a daily basis. That's especially true when it comes to sexual purity. Today we're going to look at the battlefields where we have to stand strong against temptation. Have one of the youth read the story of Tom on pages 27-28 of the book. Ask the youth for an answer to the question on page 28—Where did Tom begin to go wrong? Have them share their answer with the person sitting next to them.

The Three Battlefields: The Mind (15 minutes)

Say: The Bible says that we have to stay awake and be ready, because Satan would love to tear us down. Have one of the youth read *1 Peter 5:8* to the group. **Say: There are really three battlefields where Satan attacks us...the mind, the body, and the soul.**

Divide the youth into three groups and hand out the assignment cards. Give each group three minutes to work on their assignments. Then have the groups gather back together and report on their findings. As they share ask other youth to respond. Some sample questions: • Did anything the substance abuse group say surprise you? • Have you ever used your feelings as an excuse to do something you knew was wrong? • Any other shows or movies that you think could have a negative influence on your sexual decision-making?

Optional: This will take more time, but would be an effective way to illustrate the need to guard your mind. The week before you lead this session, tape two of your student's favorite sitcoms. Pick out one or two short scenes to show that glorify illicit sexuality. Show them following the "Sinful Habits" group. **Say: We have to keep watch for things that influence us to make lousy moral choices, even if they make us laugh or entertain us.**

The Three Battlefields: The Body (10 minutes)

Say: The second battlefield is the most obvious one: the body. But how to deal with that may not be quite as obvious. One of the "5 W's" from last session applies here...guess which one? The answer is Where, as in "Where are you going on your dates? Have youth suggest places or situations they could go on a date that wouldn't make it easy for them to give into temptation.

Have one of the youth read Psalm 1:1. **Say: Note what happens to the people mentioned in the passage. They <u>walk</u> in the counsel of the wicked, then they <u>stand</u> in the way of sinners, and finally they <u>sit</u> in the seat of mockers. They go from moving through a situation to standing still and finally to relaxing in it. We usually get comfortable with places and situations where it is easy to be tempted a step at a time, just like Tom in the story. He didn't start out planning to plant his life in the middle of the mess he created, but he chose to be in places and situations that made it easier for that to happen.** Ask the youth to think of any situations in their lives where they are starting to walk through or stand or just sit down in a tempting situation.

The Three Battlefields: The Soul (20 minutes)

Say: The final battlefield is the most important...and you can win on the other two and lose on this one. It is the battle for the soul. Have the youth read number 4 on page 25 and work on the statement below it on their own. When they finish, have two or three of the youth share their answers. **Say: God hasn't left us alone in this battle. He has promised to show us a way out, if we'll only look for it.**

Have a youth read *1 John 1:9*. **Say: Even if we mess up and get ourselves stuck in sin, God has promised to make things right. If we are Christians, we have to agree with God (that's what "confess" really means) that we sinned and need His forgiveness...and He will generously give it to us.**

Maybe you aren't sure what it means to be a Christian...or if you are, it never hurts to have a refresher course. Have the youth read through the plan of salvation on page 32-33. Have the youth you enlisted give their testimony at this time. Invite any youth who are interested in becoming a Christian to hang around after the session is over.

Closing (5 minutes)

Remind the youth of *I Corinthians 10:12*—So if you think you are standing firm, be careful that you don't fall! Encourage them to pray that God will help them stand for His glory. Have the youth pray in their groups from the earlier exercise. Have them ask God for help on the battlefields of temptation.

SESSION THREE: HOW FAR IS TOO FAR?

Stuff You Need to Do:

Enlist your creative artist and/or computer-minded youth to use their talents before the session to make the posters for the sessions.

Prepare two posters for this session. On one poster write the phrase "It's not what you're doing, it's who you're becoming." On the other poster write the phrase "God is the standard we need."

Leave the posters up from the earlier weeks. The room will become a visual reminder of the truths you are learning.

If any youth approached you last week and made a profession of faith, follow-up this week with a visit, card, or telephone call to them. Encourage them in their newfound faith.

Stuff You Need to Get:

- **10** empty two-liter cola bottles
- **skateboard**
- **chair**
- **pencils**
- **extra** Bibles

During the Session:

No Brakes (15 minutes)

Begin this session by playing "Skateboard Bowling." A hard-floored hallway or sidewalk works especially well for this game. Divide the youth into two teams. Set up the 10 two-liter bottles in a bowling pin formation at one end of the hallway. One team member sits on the skateboard and holds on while the other team members shove/push him toward the bottles. The rider cannot let go of the board until they get past the pins. Each person gets two "rolls" to knock down the pins. Let teams alternate and keep track of who knocks down the most pins. It is important that a couple of people be behind the pins and on each side of the hallway to protect the rider from crashes.

When the group finishes the game, have them read "The Brakes Don't Always Work" on page 35, and then respond to the statement. Have them share their answers with their team. **Say: The authors of the book say that once you begin riding in the immoral fast lane, you just might find out your brakes aren't fast enough. Just like the story about Rosemary or our experience with Skateboard Bowling, it's easy to get totally out of control.**

It's Not What You Do... (5 minutes)

Say: How far is too far? may not be the real important question. Point out the poster that says "It's not what you're doing, it's who you're becoming." **The issue is who you are...because who you are determines what you do. And who you are is usually a result of who you hang out with.**

He Wants to Talk (10 minutes)

Say: In light of that, it's incredible that God says clearly in the Bible that He wants to hang out with us. Give the youth five minutes to work through the exercises on developing a life of prayer on page 38. At the close of that time, lead the youth in prayer, thanking God for starting the conversation with us.

He's On Your Side (10 minutes)

Say: Not only does He want to hang out with us, He understands what we're going through. Have one of the youth read *Hebrews 4:15*. Point out that Jesus is the High Priest referred to in the passage. Have each bowling team work to rewrite *Hebrews 4:16* in their own words, then share their paraphrases with the group.

Say: God wants to talk to us, He understands what we're going through. Have one of the youth read *Hebrews 4:15*. Point out that Jesus is the High Priest referred to in the passage. Have each bowling team work to rewrite *Hebrews 4:16* in their own words, then share their paraphrases with the group.

Say: God wants to talk to us, He understands what we're going through, and He's on our side. Have one of the youth read *Hebrews 7:25*. Explain that the word *intercede* means "to ask for help on our behalf." **In other words, Jesus stands up for us.**

He Is the Standard (5 minutes)

Say: If we have a God that loves us that much, wouldn't it make sense to listen to His instructions regarding sex? Instruct the youth to read the section "Choose one Standard: God" on pages 42-43 and answer the activities.

So, How Far Is Too Far? (10 minutes)

Say: All right...we've established not only God's love for us, but also His desire for us is to control our bodies in ways that are holy and honorable. Point out that holy comes from a Greek word meaning "whole." Ask youth what being "good" morally and being whole have to do with each other. **God's love ought to define "who we are." And who we are, like we said earlier, determines what we do.**

Say: So, in the light of all we've learned today, how far is too far? Ask for a volunteer to come and stand on a chair. Have them stand in the middle of the chair and give them a light shove. Now have them stand on the edge of the chair and give them another light shove. They should come off pretty easily. **Say: Just like the person on the chair, it's easier to get out of control if we stand near the edge.** Have the youth look at the chart and the paragraph below it on page 37. **You need to choose behaviors that don't put you in danger of being out of control. The higher you are on the chart, the easier it is to put on the brakes. We've got to keep our goal in mind: to keep control of our bodies in a way that is**

holy and honorable. **Not only is it safer for us, but when we do that, we are just what** *Ephesians 5:1* **calls us to be: "imitators of God."**

Closing (5 minutes)

Have the youth read the statement "The power of God available to us . . ." on page 46. Have them write out praises to God for how He has given us His power to help us accomplish His goal of our living holy and whole lives. Give the youth about four minutes to work and have one of the youth close the group in prayer.

SESSION Four: Is Sex Wrong If You're Really in Love?

Stuff You Need to Do:

Wrap a box like a Christmas present. Put something that rattles inside it.

Create a poster of *James 1:13-15* with the same blanks as the passage printed on page 60.

Ask a female youth ahead of time to prepare to tell the story "The Theft" (p. 56) as part of the closing.

Once again, get artistic youth involved by recruiting them ahead of time to create posters of some of the sayings in the text. A couple of phrases for this session might be: "Sexual Purity—It begins in the heart and overtakes the mind" and "Too many times we focus our energy in a dating relationship on what we can't do, instead of what we can do."

Stuff You Need to Get:

- **package** of three-by-five-inch cards
- **assorted** colors of markers
- **one** piece of poster board
- **gift** wrapped box
- **pencils**
- **extra** Bibles

During the Session:

How Do You Know It's Love? (15 minutes)

Divide the youth into two teams for your own home-grown game show—"How Do You Know It's Love?" Give each team four minutes to come up with ways you can tell if you're in love and have them write each one down on a card. These can be both serious and silly. At the end of the time, mix the two team's cards together. Have a volunteer from each team compete for each card, trying to be the fastest to come up with another way to explain the card. (For example, if the card said, "You can tell you're in love if you feel butterflies in your stomach," then one of the volunteers could respond, "I feel that way when I ride roller coasters!") Give the card to the winning team. Play for about six minutes.

> **Say: You guys did a great job of questioning all the "signs" we usually use to tell if we're in love. In fact, according to the book we're using, girls fall "in love" and "out of love" an average of 10 times and guys about half that in their lives (p. 51). Think about what that would mean if you were sexually active every time you fell in love. That's not only dangerous (AIDS, pregnancy, STD's, etc.), it's an invitation to serious heartbreak.**

Have the youth read the section on pages 49-52 entitled the "Rationalization Factor." Ask for volunteers to share a time that they rationalized doing something they knew was wrong. **Say: "We're in love" is the ultimate rationalization for couples who want to be sexually active. But it's still a rationalization.**

Script Doctors (15 minutes)

Divide the youth into three groups. Assign each of the groups one of the stories on pages 52-54. Have them do the assignment on page 54 and rewrite their stories using God's standard. Have a youth read *I Thessalonians 4:3-4* to remind the group what God's standard is before they begin working on their rewrites. **Say: Just like in the movies, some stories desperately need rewriting to make them "good." That's your job...you have eight minutes to rewrite these stories and present them in our "script conference."** When the time is up, gather the youth and have each group read their rewrite.

Warning: Temptation Ahead (10 minutes)

Say: Your rewrites showed what could have happened in these stories...but how did they get out of control in the first place? Let's see what God says about that. Have a youth read the sentence on page 60 that begins: "Remember, it is not wrong to be tempted..." and have them work the Scripture exercise together as a large group. Have a volunteer fill in the blanks on the Scripture poster. Say: **Where in this process should you turn away from temptation?** Let youth answer. Ask youth what part rationalizations play in keeping us from realizing when we need to turn away.

Planning Ahead (10 minutes)

Say: **One thing that can help us stick to God's standard is good planning. I know it doesn't sound very "romantic," but neither does casual sex!** Have the youth work the exercise on page 55. Refer them to the list of activities on pages 58-59 for help in determining what kind of dates they would like to have. Point out the *Psalm 37* commitment exercise on pages 57-58 and encourage youth who are dating to work through it with their girlfriend/boyfriend.

Closing: The Gift (10 minutes)

Have the enlisted youth tell the story of "The Theft." After she finishes, show the group the box you had gift wrapped. Say: **Have you ever shaken a present to try and figure out what it was?** Shake the present. Allow youth to respond. **Have you ever torn the paper off the corner of a present to find out what it was?** Allow youth to respond. **I don't know about you, but I hated faking it on Christmas morning—pretending I was excited when I knew what it was—and I knew I had cheated. There are a lot of couples who have stolen sexual pleasure that was intended to be opened on their wedding night. Let's pray today that God will give you patience to wait and for you to not make excuses for stealing a gift that God intends to give you.** Lead the youth in prayer.

SESSION FIVE: SEX:ISN'T EVERYBODY DOING IT?

Stuff You Need to Do:

Prepare a copy of the story of Joseph that is on page 61-62 with his name changed to Joy. Start with the sentence "Like many of today's families..." and end with "though the present was full of despair." Omit the Scripture reference from Genesis.

For one last time, get artistic youth involved by recruiting them ahead of time to create posters of some of the sayings in the text. A couple of phrases for this session might be: "Live a life of NO REGRETS" and "Wait on His Best."

Stuff You Need to Get:

- *six* pieces of poster board
- *five* three-by-five-inch cards for each person
- *a piece* of paper for each person
- *assorted* colors of markers
- *pencils*
- *extra* Bibles

During the Session:

What Do You Want? (10 minutes)

Give each youth five cards and have them write one quality they want in a marriage partner on each card. When they finish, collect all of the cards and mix them together. Randomly pass out five cards to each person. Instruct them that they have three minutes to trade cards to get the cards that would best describe the person they want to marry. (They don't have to get back their own cards...they may decide someone else's idea was really good!) At the end of the time, have them to keep their top three

cards. Ask youth to share their top three with the
rest of the group.

> Say: What we just did is probably not the great-
> est process for coming up with a list of qualities
> you want in a marriage partner...but maybe it
> gave you some new ideas. Remember, it's easi-
> er to stay in control sexually if you plan ahead.
> Part of that is planning ahead for what kind of
> person you're going to marry. Encourage youth to
> take time on their own to develop a list of character
> traits and qualities they want in a mate. Offer to meet
> with them one-to-one or in small groups to work on
> these lists.

A Bible Story? (5 minutes)

Have one of the youth read the prepared story of
Joseph. Do NOT tell them this is a Bible story be-
forehand. When the youth finish, ask them if they
know anyone who has a rough family life like this.
Point out that this is really Joseph's story. Say: It
wasn't just that Joseph had great plans or
dreams to believe in...he had a great God to
believe in! And you know what? We have the
same God Joseph did!

> ### Now, For Some Good News (30 minutes)
> Say: We've spent a lot of time in the last few ses-
> sions concentrating on stories of what went
> wrong in some relationships. This time, let's focus
> on folks who have done it right.

Divide into six groups. Assign each group one of the following stories and have them answer the question(s) following it, if there are any. Then each group should create a poster that tells the rest of the groups three really

important things they learned from the passage. Give the groups about 15 minutes to work. Move from group to group, using the notes below to help provoke their thinking.

- **Deanna Hunt Carswell**
  Ask the group to think about writing these ideas down in letter form, dating them, and sealing them away until the day they get married. What an incredible gift to give to your marriage partner!

  - **Heath Thomas**
    Ask the group to explain how they could convince someone that "being a chicken" (running away) is a courageous thing to do with sexual temptation.

- **Brandon Thomas**
  Ask the group to come up with specific steps that would help them get out of a bad relationship or put the past behind them.

  - **Jason and Amy Breland**
    Ask the group to think about how praying together could be dangerous (hugging while praying turning into a makeout session, spending lots of "alone" time together, false intimacy because of spiritual closeness, etc.). Have them brainstorm ways to avoid those dangers and still get time to pray together.

- **Rafael Luciano**
  Ask the group to make sure they can explain the triangle illustration to the whole group and include it on their poster. Ask them to try to come up with another illustration of how God grows us together as we grow closer to him.

- **Chris Strack**
  Ask the group to come up with activities they could do as a group to help them remember to remain sexually pure.

At the end of the time allotted bring the groups back together and allow them plenty of time to share. Ask questions to help bring out the main points in the material. This might be a good time to share the story of Isaac waiting for the right wife, which is included in some of the group's material.

Closing and Commitment (15 minutes)

Point out the poster that says "Live a Life of No Regrets." **Say: What a way to live! Never having to look back, never wishing you'd done something different. That can start for you today. No matter where you've been or what you've done, God wants you to start today living in control. You see, He has an incredible future planned for you. Have a youth read** *Jeremiah 29:11.* **Do you really believe that?**

> Invite the youth to join you in a time of commitment. Give each person a piece of paper and have them write themselves a letter. Have them write it as if God was speaking to them. **Ask: What would God tell you to remember from what we've learned? What would He ask you to commit to?** Give them about five minutes to write their letters. If anyone is willing, let them read their letters to the group.

Close in prayer, asking God to help each youth live up to the plans God has for them. Remind them in the prayer of God's forgiveness for past sins and His desire to help them walk purely from this moment on.

CHRISTIAN GROWTH STUDY PLAN

Preparing Christians to Serve

In the Christian Growth Study Plan (formerly Church Study Course), this book **Until You Say I Do** is a resource for course credit in the subject area **Home/Family** of the Christian Growth category of diploma plans. To receive credit, read the book, complete the learning activities, show your work to your pastor, a staff member or church leader, then complete the information on the next page. The form may be duplicated. Send the completed page to:

**Christian Growth
Study Plan
127 Ninth Avenue, North,
MSN 117
Nashville, TN 37234-0117
FAX: (615)251-5067**

For information about the Christian Growth Study Plan, refer to the current Christian Growth Study Plan Catalog. Your church office may have a copy. If not, request a free copy from the Christian Growth Study Plan office (615/251-2525).

Until You Say I Do CG-0211

PARTICIPANT INFORMATION

Social Security Number (USA ONLY)

Personal CGSP Number*

Date of Birth (MONTH, DAY, YEAR)

Name (First, Middle, Last)
☐ Mr. ☐ Miss
☐ Mrs.

Home Phone

Address (Street, Route, or P.O. Box)

City, State, or Province

Zip/Postal Code

CHURCH INFORMATION

Church Name

Address (Street, Route, or P.O. Box)

City, State, or Province

Zip/Postal Code

CHANGE REQUEST ONLY

☐ Former Name

☐ Former Address

City, State, or Province

Zip/Postal Code

☐ Former Church

City, State, or Province

Zip/Postal Code

Signature of Pastor, Conference Leader, or Other Church Leader

Date

*New participants are requested but not required to give SS# and date of birth. Existing participants, please give CGSP# when using SS# for the first time. Thereafter, only one ID# is required. Mail to: Christian Growth Study Plan, 127 Ninth Ave., North, Nashville, TN 37234-0117. Fax: (615)251-5067